NML/FF

Please return / renew by date shown.
You can renew at: **norlink.norfolk.gov.uk**
or by telephone: **0344 800 8006**
Please have you library card & PIN ready

NORFOLK LIBRARY
AND INFORMATION SERVICE

D1375001

ROBERT HERRICK
Poems selected by STEPHEN ROMER

faber and faber

First published in 2010
by Faber and Faber Limited
Bloomsbury House, 74–77 Great Russell Street
London WC1B 3DA

Typeset by RefineCatch Ltd, Bungay, Suffolk
Printed in England by CPI Bookmarque, Croydon

A CIP record for this book
is available from the British Library

ISBN 978–0–571–23680–0

10 9 8 7 6 5 4 3 2 1

Contents

Introduction

1

Is Robert Herrick the happiest of our poets? He is certainly
sweet-tempered, both in humour and in harmony, and like
his great contemporary and fellow West Country clergyman,
George Herbert, he delighted in music and song. Herrick
was one of those blessed with an enduring pleasure in small,
fleeting things, in trifles, in silks and tiffanies, in festivals and
merry-making, drinking and 'wassailing'. Among the instantly
endearing things about this poet is his desire to give *us*, his
readers, pleasure too. In one of many poems on 'His Book'
he stipulates that he would have it read only in the evening,
by a spitting fire, after a hearty meal and a good few drinks –
for then 'rigid Cato' (the Roman censor) would be more indul-
gent. But there is a caveat – if we do not care for *any* of his
wares – and there is after all a wide selection on offer – then, like
his 'Soure reader', we are roundly to be cursed: 'The Extreame
Scabbe take thee, and thine, for me.' In context, the 'Perverse
Man' of his censure must also be the Puritan, since *Hesperides*
is the least puritanical of books, given over as most of it is to
wine, women and song. The pious *Noble Numbers* at the end – a
slim and rather anxious reminder of his day-job as a country
parson – hardly provide the counterweight that, say, Donne's
Divine Poems do for his profane *Songs & Sonets*. It is likely
that Herrick's religious poems were added – and this gives
a true flavour of those intense, peculiar times – as a selling
point for the book: it was religious controversy that shifted
copies in the 1630s and throughout the Civil War. Political
or religious polemic was never Herrick's strong suit, and he
did not pretend otherwise. An uncritical, some would say
unthinking, Royalist, his praise of Charles can look excessive.
But he was a Cavalier through and through, a lover of good and
gracious living, the most Elizabethan of the Jacobeans – and

it would be a sour reader indeed that condemned him for these things.

Yeats's image of Keats as a 'schoolboy with his face and nose pressed to the sweet-shop window' seems entirely applicable to Herrick as well. He says in 'The Argument of his Book' that he sings, among other things, 'Of Bride-grooms, Brides, and of their Bridall-cakes', the third element carrying apparently the same weight for the poet as the first two. Perhaps it is this quality in Herrick – the utter predictability of his tastes, his delight in pretty women, his frank enjoyment of drink and male company (Ben Jonson's 'lyrick feasts'), his love of festivals, his due respect for death, his acceptance of the status quo, his unrevolutionary politics, his alternating cravings for the stimulus of the city and for rural peace– that Eliot was referring to when he spoke of Herrick's 'endearing *ordinariness* . . .' While looking like a typically back-handed compliment, the judgement is in fact spot-on. We should not look to him for the seriousness and learning of a Jonson, nor for the intellectual subtlety or the grand rhetorical gestures of a Donne, nor for the single-minded godliness and purpose of a Herbert, nor for the metaphysical curiosity and political astutenes of a Marvell. A minor poet, then? Without starting that hare, we can accept that he is a lighter poet than these former, and his range is narrower. Often, however, his lyrics are any match for theirs: the best of them will last as long as the language. What he himself describes as his 'wanton cleanlinesse' might be likened to wholesomeness, and Herrick is finally a wholesome poet, not in the least perverse. 'Where Care/None is, slight things do lightly please,' he says in the touching poem of retirement 'His Grange, or private wealth'. A renewable delight in small things is itself a kind of genius.

He was born in Cheapside, London in 1591 into a prosperous middle-class family of goldsmiths, originally of Leicestershire stock. The previous year, Spenser had published *The Faerie Queene*, Sidney his *Arcadia*, Shakespeare was writing *Richard III* and Elizabeth Gloriana was on the throne. When he died, aged eighty-three, Dryden was already Poet Laureate. Herrick lived under four monarchs, survived the Civil War and the Commonwealth, welcomed the Restoration, and died peacefully in his rectory at Dean Prior, Devonshire in October 1674, the same year as Milton. The contrast is instructive, between the public and the private, the lyric and the epic poet. The impress of 'public events' is everywhere felt in Milton's work and career, almost nowhere in Herrick's, apart from two poems addressed to the 'Untuneable' and to the 'Troublesome' Times respectively. The image of Herrick as essentially an apolitical animal has, it is true, been challenged in recent scholarship. Some have discerned a more deliberate religious and political polemic in *Hesperides* than previously acknowledged, with evidence of support for the ritualism of Archbishop Laud. Be that as it may, the whole spirit of *Hesperides* does not strike me as polemical. Rather, it is deeply conservative, and when not harking back to some golden Helicon, it seems to embrace the status quo. That said, in the peculiar context of Puritanism, celebrating the Maypole or the harvest festival could look like political acts. The most explicitly political poems in Herrick's book are those addressed to Charles, and they are the poems of a devout subject who seems to share that king's exacerbated sense of his divine right. We are a long way from Milton! And the contrast serves to illuminate the terrible, fratricidal, antagonism of the time, when the very idea of England was at stake.

When Robert Herrick was but one year old a personal tragedy struck the family quite as hard as any public event: on 7 November 1592, his father Nicholas made his will, and two days later he fell to his death from an upper window of his house in Cheapside. It is assumed, though it was never proved, that he committed suicide. Fortunately for the family, enough doubt surrounded the incident to prevent the Crown from seizing Nicholas's assets, normally forfeited in those days in the case of suicide. This bizarre fact does not seem to have marked the poet unduly, and indeed seems quite out of family character, for the Herricks were in general a sanguine, long-lived lot. The family, and Robert in particular, came under the protection of a kindly uncle, Sir William. It was he who took the poet on as apprentice in the family business, and – when it became clear that Robert would never make a master goldsmith – he who financed his studies at Cambridge. Clearly, however, the family passion for fine and curious workmanship was not lost on Robert, it was simply transfered to fashioning patterns out of words. While, as we shall see, he prizes a slight disorder in the dress as the final stroke of beauty, he is himself a supreme artificer. And if we love Herrick now for the freshness of his daffodils and his violets, he also possesses the Baroque fascination for complexity – the praise of glass and crystal casings, to offset beauty in flowers, in 'The Lilly in the Christal' is a good example. It reads a little like a flower-setter's manual. Allied to this is the undisguised delight in the exotic words for jewels and scents – the 'Topaz, Opal, Calcedon', the Pomander, Spikenard and Amber-Greece – that are scattered in the poems to his 'mistresses'. There is also the Herrick hallmark on the English language itself – I have found two coinages attributed to him in the *OED*: 'Time's *trans-shifting*' in the inaugural poem of *Hesperides*, and the noble praise of Julia's breasts as 'circummortall'. It is as though the language, as yet unfixed and standardized by Johnson's *Dictionary*, were still a glorious magma from which poets could fashion, like metalworkers, newfangled words.

And so to Cambridge, first for a year's carousing and over-spending at St John's – Herrick employs every rhetorical trick in the book to extract more money from Sir William, in a rather touching stream of letters that have come down to us. They begin almost on arrival, with the correspondent dismayed at having arrived at the great seat of learning without 'bedding'. After a year he removed to the smaller, apparently more sober, but still beautiful Trinity Hall, down the road, for four years of Law. He explained to Sir William: 'I purpose to live recluse . . . striving now with my self (retayning upright thoughts) both sparingly to live, thereby to shun the current of expence . . .' He seems to have held good, and took his BA in 1617, his MA in 1620.

But instead of practising at the Bar, he was ordained Deacon alongside his good friend John Weekes in 1623, and (quite irregularly) ordained priest in the Church of England the very next day by the Bishop of Peterborough. Next to nothing is known of his movements (there are major gaps in our knowledge of Herrick's life) during the London years of the 1620s. From the internal evidence of the poems, it is clear he frequented Ben Jonson, and the court musicians (who set some of his poems) William and Henry Lawes. As an assistant chaplain he accompanied the Duke of Buckingham on his catastrophic campaign to the Ile de Ré, to help the French Huguenots in 1627. He was appointed to the living of Dean Prior in south Devonshire in 1629, a post he finally took up in 1630, the very same month that George Herbert became rector of Bemerton in Wiltshire. It is clear that Herrick was known as a poet by 1625, when the author of the *Muses Dirge*, speaking of the death of King James, wonders why 'some Jonson, Drayton, or some Herrick' has not penned a worthy elegy to mark the event. As it turned out, this was the highest praise Herrick was to receive in his lifetime; and it is significant he is placed alongside two great Elizabethans, for in a sense he outlived both his age and the taste it created.

Apart from a period of enforced return to London during the Commonwealth (a fact he welcomes ecstatically in his poem to mark the occasion), Herrick spent the rest of his days either content or dull as vicar of the country parish of Dean Prior in 'lothèd Devonshire'. His single volume of poems, his belovèd Book, *Hesperides*, in which he invested himself so entirely, was published in St Paul's Churchyard, London, in 1648, to a deafening silence.

2

When the Revd Robert Herrick stepped out of his vicarage at Dean Prior, he seemed to step less into the English countryside than into a Christian-Pagan Arcadia. Apollo's lyre hangs from a tree, and young ladies with names out of classical Rome flit among the bosky groves. But here and there are the wild flowers of England, and cherry blossom, and whitethorn with which to deck the halls in May. His remote English vicarage is part that, and part Horace's villa in the Sabine Hills above Rome. The easy blend of Christian and pagan, the classical learning that runs so deep (adaptations of Horace, Catullus, Ovid, Martial and others are ubiquitous in *Hesperides*), is in effect part of the furniture of Renaissance humanism. But the poet who showed Herrick how to put these classical sources to effect in English was of course that uniquely learned and impressive self-made scholar Ben Jonson, 'the rare Arch-Poet'. Although he was never officially a member of the Tribe of Ben, Herrick's repeated poems of praise to his master are among his most generous and heartfelt; they go beyond mere sycophancy. They also provide us with crucial insights into that missing decade, a lot of which was spent in Ben's 'Lyrick Feasts/Made at the *Sun*/The *Dog*, the triple *Tunne*' ('An Ode for him'). More revealing still is 'His Prayer to Ben. Johnson':

> When I a Verse shall make,
> Know I have praid thee,
> For old Religions sake,
> Saint Ben to aide me.

This, one feels, is no idle invocation to a (rather unorthodoxly classical) saint: among many things that Herrick learned from his Master was the importance of ceaseless revision – and the successive versions of certain poems from *Hesperides* show that the lesson was not lost on the pupil.

What Thom Gunn has said of Jonson's classicism – 'it is not merely a question of bringing Martial or Juvenal up to date, nor even of building up a national literature that can rival the classics, it is a matter of continuing the life and society that was behind the literature, evaluating, adapting, naturalizing it' – is a matter of instinct for Herrick, and the very pulse of his art. He *begins* with the world of 'order and Disposure', of rank and social hierarchy: this is the solid ground from which he can launch his imaginative sallies and flirtations. And it is fitting therefore, that what is perhaps his most interesting theme should have been suggested by a fragment in one of Jonson's plays, the 'Song' from *Epicoene* that contains the lines 'Robes loosely flowing, haire as free: Such sweet neglect more taketh me,/Than all th'adulteries of art.' This in Herrick's hands becomes the small masterpiece 'Delight in Disorder', which concludes:

A carelesse shooe-string, in whose tye
I see a wilde civility:
Doe more bewitch me, then when Art
Is too precise in every part.

The wild civility of the shoelace carelessly tied shows us Herrick the complete Cavalier, with a roving eye for silken clothes, the stray curl, the loose riband, the 'tempestuous petticote', but it is a formula he returns to often, this wild civility or, when he reverses the terms, this 'civil wilderness'. It is related to the Shakespearean debate between the contested merits of natural and grafted, or hybrid flowers: in what consists nature, and what artifice, and can artifice 'improve' upon nature? I have already described Herrick as a supreme artificer, so despite his predilection for 'delight in disorder', there seem to be two poems that counter the proposition, by reversing it. 'Art above Nature, to Julia' is an elegant way of saying that the woman artfully clothed is more alluring than the woman naked:

Next, when those Lawnie Filmes I see
Play with a wild civility:
And all those airie silks to flow,
Alluring me, and tempting so:
I must confesse, mine eye and heart
Dotes less on Nature, then on Art.

And in 'What kind of Mistresse he would have' he asks that she be:

Pure enough, though not Precise:
Be she shewing, in her dresse,
Like a civill Wilderness;
That the curious may detect
Order in a sweet neglect . . .

She must in all cases, in fact, preserve a Horatian *via media* between order and neglect, between restraint and passion. Perhaps we can extend the analogy to say that Herrick desires not a Civil War, nor a Puritan Commonalty, but a Civil Wilderness, an orderly, hierarchical civilisation that leaves a place for the ancient, the pagan, the instinctive – in a word, for the body. And for the traditional function of festival, as a temporary outlet for the lord of misrule: the Bacchanalia or the Lupercalia. It is this need, whether articulated consciously or not, that finds expression in the Cavalier imitations of the boozing songs of Anacreon.

Herrick is emphatically pre-Romantic, but is it fanciful to see, in his 'delight in disorder', in the 'tempestuous petticote' of his mistress, the first flash of Elizabeth Bennet's muddy hem, which is surely the precise, polite equivalent in Jane Austen? And in Julia's sweet 'disorder', may we not see a first flowering of the English rose, the beauty who combines elegance with naturalness, naturalness with elegance?

The same ideal is surely at the heart of what is probably Herrick's most accomplished single poem, 'Corinna's going a Maying', whose elaborate stanzas synthesise in one gloriously felicitous expression the essence of his universe. Corinna, an English rose with a pagan name, steps out from her Anglican orisons ('be briefe in praying') into an English Helicon of delicious freshness, where the goddess Flora presides over the bright young things on their festive day out. Corinna is urged to come forth from her chamber, and not to bother to over-adorn herself (and here is that civil wilderness) because 'leaves will strew/ Gemms in abundance upon you'. The natural world, that is, provides the sufficient ornament (he repeats the theme in the small, perfect lyric 'Upon Julia's haire fill'd with Dew'). Corinna's poem goes on to enumerate the May-day celebration in pointedly anti-Puritan vein (and the pointedness must be deliberate – here at least I would agree with recent readings that find in Herrick a more deliberately political and polemical stance than hitherto allowed); kisses are exchanged, greengowns given – bashful lasses were (chastely or otherwise) rolled over in the grass by their swain – and troths are plighted. But in the last stanza, where Herrick rises magnificently to his favourite theme of *Carpe diem*, we have writing whose stateliness rivals that of Marvell or Donne. He uses his classical sources (Horace and Catullus) to triumphant effect in English:

> Come, let us goe, while we are in our prime;
> And take the harmlesse follie of the time.
> We shall grow old apace, and die
> Before we know our liberty.
> Our life is short; and our dayes run
> As fast away as do's the Sunne:
> And as a vapour, or a drop of raine
> Once lost, can ne'er be found againe . . .

It will not do, however, to make Herrick out as a kind of precursor of the Romantics in his taste for the artfully careless, or lightly windswept; in a further usage of the oxymoron that seems to have bewitched him, when contemplating Julia's elaborate dress and the 'Lawnie Filmes' that play about her 'with a wild civility', he concludes that the charming wantonness of her clothes leaves him doting 'less on Nature, than on Art'.

If elegance with naturalness (or Delight in Disorder) is one of the most interesting cruxes in Herrick today, there is a great deal of what I suppose is the seventeenth-century equivalent of bodice-ripping – ruby lips and alabaster thighs and creamy breasts – the Petrarchan inventory, the Spenserean catalogue, the French *blasons du corps féminin*. The kind of thing that Shakespeare mocked in 'My mistress' eyes are nothing like the sun'. And it is here that a glass screen comes down, separating us, incurable post-Romantics that we are, from the imaginative world of the seventeenth century. Robert Herrick disappears into a looking-glass world whose conventions we cannot understand, whose delights we cannot share. Much the same has been said of our attitude to the Shakespearean pun, especially after Samuel Johnson's censure. To us, these *concetti* give off such a whiff of artificiality (the opposite of Lizzie's hem) they can only be appreciated as a kind of period kitsch. And only in very limited doses: accordingly, my selection goes easy on them. Some I have kept in, if only because, when true to form, he can take the similes to hilariously ludicrous extremes, the girls in question becoming little more than curvaceous, ambulant dairies, as in 'Wo'd yee have fresh Cheese and Cream? Julia's Breast can give you them . . .' – topped off, needless to say, with a dash of strawberry nipple.

The ladies themselves, those fleeting lovely muses, that *escadron volant* of classical beauties, leaving a trace of spikenard or ambergris on the air, have no more existence than the fantasmal mistresses of another confirmed bachelor, Horace. Dianeme, Perilla, Anthea, Sylvia, Phyllis, Electra and the rest are simply ciphers in various states of sweet undress. It should be quickly evident that Herrick is all about flirtation and foreplay, he is devoted, in John Creaser's word, to 'indirection', to 'toying and talking'. His generalisations about women – that their bashfulness is artful, that no means yes – are merely of their period. There is no biographical evidence that Julia, his favourite, and the recipient of some of his loveliest verse, existed; one likes to imagine that she is based on a woman of wit and beauty, the seventeenth-century equivalent of a Mme Récamier, whom Herrick might have met, and admired from afar, in the safety of a crowd. Or perhaps, who knows, more intimately, during his early years in London. There must have been women around during Ben Jonson's 'lyrick feasts' in the London taverns, though whether Julia, who seems decidedly superior with her silks and her sweet singing voice, would have frequented them is another matter. Perhaps after all Robert Herrick was a shy man in these matters, underneath all the Anacreontic roistering and banter. He may also have been unhappy with his looks. Certainly, the evidence of the Marshall engraving that adorned the frontispiece of *Hesperides* is not encouraging; with its bull neck, thin moustache, crook nose, and snaking black curls, his profile rises up from a rather monstrous plinth, with a background of pagan hills and clustered cupids. His biographer Marchette Chute describes his appearance nicely as something between 'a minor Roman emperor and a prosperous English butcher.'

Herrick is also fastidious in his tastes: the cruel bite of his epigrams comes as something of a surprise – the mocking jibe at the infirmities of others shows a puerile side to our poet. Some of them are very funny, all the same. This genre also has its source in the classics, filtered once again through the example of Ben Jonson. Epigrams are scattered liberally throughout *Hesperides*, often intruding like a coarse, clownish nose between two lovely lyrics, and that is how I have kept the few I have included, for they are the sour to the sweet, and Herrick surely intended the mixture of the two. Bad teeth, bad breath, blemished skin draw his acid censure, and that is only the start. One remarkable fact is that 'Scobble', who 'whips his wife for whoredom', and 'Glasco', proud of his false teeth made of mutton bone, were names the vicar of Dean Prior took from his own parish register, as if in revenge on the 'currish' and 'churlish' manners of the countryfolk that made up his flock, and to whom he could never be quite reconciled. This is all in stark contrast to the diligent effort at charitable tolerance, patience and education counselled by George Herbert in *The Country Parson*.

More appealing, and certainly tenderer, are the poems in praise of the country life (again, the tradition here is a long one). Herrick's have a special charm, because he fills them with homely detail (his maid Prew, his spaniel Trasy, his pet Lamb, his goose, his hen, his cat, are all named in 'His Grange, his wealth'). These alternate with the lament at his fate, at being stuck in 'dull' or 'lothèd' Devonshire, five days of hard riding on bad roads from London. But he does admit, early on, that his enforced retirement, *hic in reducta valle*, has given him the leisure to write more 'Ennobled numbers' than ever before. Otherwise, the only external record, or rumour, that we have of Herrick's behaviour as the incumbent of Dean Prior is that he once flung his sermon at his congregation, in disgust at their inattention. One suspects, though, the people in return tolerated him as a kindly, if eccentric figure, a single gent who employed a much-loved housekeeper, Prew Baldwin (he took her back after he regained his living at the Restoration), and who kept a range of pets, including a pig he trained to drink from a tankard. Thirty years after his death, it is recorded that there was an illiterate old lady left in the village who recalled Herrick and still recited some of his *Noble Numbers* at bedtime.

3

Herrick was born, and St John of the Cross died, in 1591. Far from suggesting any transmigration of souls, it is rather the incongruity of this singular fact that raises a smile. For one thing, it is a reminder that poetry has many mansions, for there is a gulf separating the spiritual experience of the two men. St John was an ascetic who knew the Dark Night of the Soul, Herrick an easy-going Anglican cleric whose theology, while elegantly turned in *Noble Numbers*, is of the fairly basic, Sunday-school variety. What it lacks, compared to that of the Spaniard, or of Donne or Herbert, is any strong sense of the personal *vécu*. The 'Employment' and 'Affliction' poems of Herbert are a cry *de profundis* that reverberates through to us with total clarity; a Romantic like Coleridge heard it clearly, and echoed it, in 'Work without Hope'. Similarly, we treasure 'The Flower' as a sublime testament of personal faith and renewal, as we do Donne's 'Nocturnall' for its lived anguish. I am not saying that we moderns can only appreciate the personal confession, but there is an obliquity, a reticence in Herrick (despite all the poems 'To Himself') that makes him, finally, a remoter figure. What Eliot found lacking in *Hesperides* was the 'continuous conscious purpose' he found in Herbert's *The Temple*, but I suspect he also missed any sense of urgent personal trajectory. *Pace* those who have tried to invent a unity to *Hesperides*, the only unity it has – but it is the perfect one for the job – is *anno domini*, the poet gets older, and prepares increasingly for the grave – and his Book for an immortality he never doubts. It is also perhaps a reason for his delay in publishing it. He was fifty-seven when it eventually appeared.

And yet there are poems of Herrick's in which another voice seems to emerge, one that possesses a different personal accent – the poems of country life are among them, with their genial and anecdotal matter. A masterpiece like 'To Meddows' has a melancholy and a local flavour that transcends its sources. I would also hold up for special mention 'The comming of good luck', a breathtaking quatrain that reveals this personal note in Herrick:

> So Good-luck came, and on my roofe did light,
> Like noyse-lesse Snow; or as the dew of night:
> Not all at once, but gently, as the trees
> Are, by the Sun-beams, tickel'd by degrees.

The meaning here is delayed by the syntax, which slows and picks up and slows again, in a way perfectly matched to the poem's subject, which is in itself unusual. This is the word-perfect work of a master, a poet of immense tact, with an immaculate ear. Swinburne, hyperbolic as ever, called him the 'greatest songwriter – as surely as Shakespeare is the greatest dramatist – ever born of English race'. Elizabeth Barrett Browning called him, aptly, 'the Ariel of poets, sucking "where the bee sucks"', and it is true that his poems on blossoms and flowers bring Shakespeare's lyrics strongly to mind. Another poet-priest, though of a rather different stripe, Gerard Manley Hopkins, once wrote in passing of Herrick and Herbert, associating them with 'the smell of oxeyes and applelofts'. There is about Herrick's poetry a 'dearest freshness', and an inviolable felicity.

STEPHEN ROMER

ROBERT HERRICK

The Argument of his Book

I sing of Brooks, of Blossomes, Birds, and Bowers:
Of April, May, of June, and July-Flowers.
I sing of May-poles, Hock-carts, Wassails, Wakes,
Of Bride-grooms, Brides, and of their Bridall-cakes.
I write of Youth, of Love, and have Accesse
By these, to sing of cleanly-Wantonnesse.
I sing of Dewes, of Raines, and piece by piece
Of Balme, of Oyle, of Spice, and Amber-Greece.
I sing of Times trans-shifting; and I write
How Roses first came Red, and Lillies White.
I write of Groves, of Twilights, and I sing
The Court of Mab, and of the Fairie-King.
I write of Hell; I sing (and ever shall)
Of Heaven, and hope to have it after all.

To his Muse

Whither Mad maiden wilt thou roame?
Farre safer 'twere to stay at home:
Where thou mayst sit, and piping please
The poore and private Cottages.
Since Coats, and Hamlets, best agree
With this thy meaner Minstralsie.
There with the Reed, thou mayst expresse
The Shepherds Fleecie happinesse:
And with thy Eclogues intermixe
Some smooth, and harmlesse Beucolicks.
There on a Hillock thou mayst sing
Unto a handsome Shephardling;
Or to a Girle (that keeps the Neat)
With breath more sweet then Violet.
There, there, (perhaps) such Lines as These
May take the simple Villages.
But for the Court, the Country wit
Is despicable unto it.
Stay then at home, and doe not goe
Or flie abroad to seeke for woe.
Contempts in Courts and Cities dwell;
No Critick haunts the Poore mans Cell:
Where thou mayst hear thine own Lines read
By no one tongue, there, censured.
That man's unwise will search for Ill,
And may prevent it, sitting still.

To his Booke

While thou didst keep thy Candor undefil'd,
Deerely I lov'd thee; as my first-borne child:
But when I saw thee wantonly to roame
From house to house, and never stay at home;
I brake my bonds of Love, and bad thee goe,
Regardlesse whether well thou sped'st, or no.
On with thy fortunes then, what e're they be;
If good I'le smile, if bad I'le sigh for Thee.

Another

To read my Booke the Virgin shie
May blush, (while Brutus standeth by:)
But when He's gone, read through what's writ,
And never staine a cheeke for it.

Another

Who with thy leaves shall wipe (at need)
The place, where swelling Piles do breed:
May every Ill, that bites, or smarts,
Perplexe him in his hinder-parts.

To the soure Reader

If thou dislik'st the Piece thou light'st on first;
Thinke that of All, that I have writ, the worst:
But if thou read'st my Booke unto the end,
And still do'st this, and that verse, reprehend:
O Perverse man! If All disgustfull be,
The Extreame Scabbe take thee, and thine, for me.

When he would have his verses read

In sober mornings, doe not thou reherse
The holy incantation of a verse;
But when that men have both well drunke, and fed,
Let my Enchantments then be sung, or read.
When Laurell spirts 'ith fire, and when the Hearth
Smiles to it selfe, and guilds the roofe with mirth;
When up the Thyrse is rais'd, and when the sound
Of sacred Orgies flyes, A round, A round.
When the Rose raignes, and locks with ointments shine,
Let rigid Cato read these Lines of mine.

Upon Julias Recovery

Droop, droop no more, or hang the head
Ye Roses almost withered;
Now strength, and newer Purple get,
Each here declining Violet.
O Primroses! let this day be
A Resurrection unto ye;
And to all flowers ally'd in blood,
Or sworn to that sweet Sister-hood:
For Health on Julia's cheek hath shed
Clarret, and Creame commingled.
And those her lips doe now appeare
As beames of Corrall, but more cleare.

The Parliament of Roses to Julia

I dreamt the Roses one time went
To meet and sit in Parliament:
The place for these, and for the rest
Of flowers, was thy spotlesse breast:
Over the which a State was drawne
Of Tiffanie, or Cob-web Lawne;
Then in that Parly, all those powers
Voted the Rose; the Queen of flowers.
But so, as that her self should be
The maide of Honour unto thee.

To Perenna

When I thy Parts runne o're, I can't espie
In any one, the least indecencie:
But every Line, and Limb diffused thence,
A faire, and unfamiliar excellence:
So, that the more I look, the more I prove,
Ther's still more cause, why I the more should love.

To his Mistresses

Helpe me! helpe me! now I call
To my pretty Witchcrafts all:
Old I am, and cannot do
That, I was accustom'd to.
Bring your Magicks, Spels, and Charmes,
To enflesh my thighs, and armes:
Is there no way to beget
In my limbs their former heat?
Æson had (as Poets faine)
Baths that made him young againe:
Find that Medicine (if you can)
For your drie-decrepid man:
Who would faine his strength renew,
Were it but to pleasure you.

No Loathsomnesse in love

What I fancy, I approve,
No Dislike there is in love:
Be my Mistresse short or tall,
And distorted there-withall:
Be she likewise one of those,
That an Acre hath of Nose:
Be her forehead, and her eyes
Full of incongruities:
Be her cheeks so shallow too,
As to shew her Tongue wag through:
Be her lips ill hung, or set,
And her grinders black as jet;
Ha's she thinne haire, hath she none,
She's to me a Paragon.

The Weeping Cherry

I saw a Cherry weep, and why?
   Why wept it? but for shame,
Because my Julia's lip was by,
   And did out-red the same.
But pretty Fondling, let not fall
   A teare at all for that:
Which Rubies, Corralls, Scarlets, all
   For tincture, wonder at.

Soft Musick

The mellow touch of musick most doth wound
The soule, when it doth rather sigh, then sound.

The Difference Betwixt Kings and Subjects

Twixt Kings and Subjects ther's this mighty odds,
Subjects are taught by Men; Kings by the Gods.

No Spouse but a Sister

A Bachelour I will
Live as I have liv'd still,
And never take a wife
To crucifie my life:
But this I'le tell ye too,
What now I meane to doe;
A Sister (in the stead
Of Wife) about I'le lead;
Which I will keep embrac'd,
And kisse, but yet be chaste.

The shooe tying

Anthea bade me tye her shooe;
I did; and kist the Instep too:
And would have kist unto her knee,
Had not her Blush rebuked me.

The Carkanet

Instead of Orient Pearls, of Jet,
I sent my Love a Karkanet:
About her spotlesse neck she knit
The lace, to honour me, or it:
Then think how wrapt was I to see
My Jet t'enthrall such Ivorie.

His sailing from Julia

When that day comes, whose evening sayes I'm gone
Unto that watrie Desolation:
Devoutly to thy Closet-gods then pray,
That my wing'd Ship may meet no Remora.
Those Deities which circum-walk the Seas,
And look upon our dreadfull passages,
Will from all dangers, re-deliver me,
For one drink-offering, poured out by thee.
Mercie and Truth live with thee! and forbeare
(In my short absence) to unsluce a teare:
But yet for Loves-sake, let thy lips doe this,
Give my dead picture one engendring kisse:
Work that to life, and let me ever dwell
In thy remembrance (Julia.) So farewell.

How the Wall-flower came first, and why so called

Why this Flower is now call'd so,
List' sweet maids, and you shal know.
Understand, this First-ling was
Once a brisk and bonny Lasse,
Kept as close as Danae was:
Who a sprightly Springall lov'd,
And to have it fully prov'd,
Up she got upon a wall,
Tempting down to slide withall:
But the silken twist unty'd,
So she fell, and bruis'd, she dy'd.
Love, in pitty of the deed,
And her loving-lucklesse speed,
Turn'd her to this Plant, we call
Now, The Flower of the Wall.

Why Flowers change colour

These fresh beauties (we can prove)
Once were Virgins sick of love,
Turn'd to Flowers. Still in some
Colours goe, and colours come.

The Vision to Electra

I dream'd we both were in a bed
Of Roses, almost smothered:
The warmth and sweetnes had me there
Made lovingly familiar:
But that I heard thy sweet breath say,
Faults done by night, will blush by day:
I kist thee (panting,) and I call
Night to the Record! that was all.
But ah! if empty dreames so please,
Love give me more such nights as these.

His request to Julia

Julia, if I chance to die
Ere I print my Poetry;
I most humbly thee desire
To commit it to the fire:
Better 'twere my Book were dead,
Then to live not perfected.

Upon Julia's Voice

So smooth, so sweet, so silv'ry is thy voice,
As, could they hear, the Damn'd would make no noise,
But listen to thee, (walking in thy chamber)
Melting melodious words, to Lutes of Amber.

The succession of the foure sweet months

First, April, she with mellow showrs
Opens the way for early flowers;
Then after her comes smiling May,
In a more rich and sweet aray:
Next enters June, and brings us more
Jems, then those two, that went before:
Then (lastly) July comes, and she
More wealth brings in, then all those three.

No Shipwrack of Vertue. To a friend

Thou sail'st with others, in this Argus here;
Nor wrack, or Bulging thou hast cause to feare:
But trust to this, my noble passenger;
Who swims with Vertue, he shall still be sure
(Ulysses-like) all tempests to endure;
And 'midst a thousand gulfs to be secure.

Of Love. A Sonet

How Love came in, I do not know,
Whether by th'eye, or eare, or no:
Or whether with the soule it came
(At first) infused with the same:
Whether in part 'tis here or there,
Or, like the soule, whole every where:
This troubles me: but I as well
As any other, this can tell;
That when from hence she does depart,
The out-let then is from the heart.

To Anthea

Ah my Anthea! Must my heart still break?
(Love makes me write, what shame forbids to speak.)
Give me a kisse, and to that kisse a score;
Then to that twenty, adde an hundred more:
A thousand to that hundred: so kisse on,
To make that thousand up a million.
Treble that million, and when that is done,
Let's kisse afresh, as when we first begun.
But yet, though Love likes well such Scenes as these,
There is an Act that will more fully please:
Kissing and glancing, soothing, all make way
But to the acting of this private Play:
Name it I would; but being blushing red,
The rest Ile speak, when we meet both in bed.

To the King, Upon his comming with his Army into the West

Welcome, most welcome to our Vowes and us,
Most great, and universall Genius!
The Drooping West, which hitherto has stood
As one, in long-lamented-widow-hood;
Looks like a Bride now, or a bed of flowers,
Newly refresh't, both by the Sun, and showers.
War, which before was horrid, now appears
Lovely in you, brave Prince of Cavaliers!
A deale of courage in each bosome springs
By your accesse; (O you the best of Kings!)
Ride on with all white Omens; so, that where
Your Standard's up, we fix a Conquest there.

To the King and Queene, upon their unhappy distances

Woe, woe to them, who (by a ball of strife)
Doe, and have parted here a Man and Wife:
CHARLS the best Husband, while MARIA strives
To be, and is, the very best of Wives:
Like Streams, you are divorc'd; but 'twill come, when
These eyes of mine shall see you mix agen.
Thus speaks the Oke, here; C. and M. shall meet,
Treading on Amber, with their silver-feet:
Nor wil't be long, ere this accomplish'd be;
The words found true, C. M. remember me.

Dangers wait on Kings

As oft as Night is banish'd by the Morne,
So oft, we'll think, we see a King new born.

The Cheat of Cupid:
or, The ungentle guest

One silent night of late,
    When every creature rested,
Came one unto my gate,
    And knocking, me molested.

Who's that (said I) beats there,
    And troubles thus the Sleepie?
Cast off (said he) all feare,
    And let not Locks thus keep ye.

For I a Boy am, who
    By Moonlesse nights have swerved;
And all with showrs wet through,
    And e'en with cold half starved.

I pittifull arose,
    And soon a Taper lighted;
And did my selfe disclose
    Unto the lad benighted.

I saw he had a Bow,
    And Wings too, which did shiver;
And looking down below,
    I spy'd he had a Quiver.

I to my Chimney's shine
    Brought him, (as Love professes)
And chaf'd his hands with mine,
    And dry'd his dropping Tresses:

But when he felt him warm'd,
    Let's try this bow of ours,
And string if they be harm'd,
    Said he, with these late showrs.

Forthwith his bow he bent,
  And wedded string and arrow,
And struck me that it went
  Quite through my heart and marrow.

Then laughing loud, he flew
  Away, and thus said flying,
Adieu, mine Host, Adieu,
  Ile leave thy heart a dying.

To the reverend shade of his religious Father

That for seven Lusters I did never come
To doe the Rites to thy Religious Tombe:
That neither haire was cut, or true teares shed
By me, o'r thee, (as justments to the dead)
Forgive, forgive me; since I did not know
Whether thy bones had here their Rest, or no.
But now 'tis known, Behold; behold, I bring
Unto thy Ghost, th'Effused Offering:
And look, what Smallage, Night-shade, Cypresse, Yew,
Unto the shades have been, or now are due,
Here I devote; And something more then so;
I come to pay a Debt of Birth I owe.
Thou gav'st me life, (but Mortall;) For that one
Favour, Ile make full satisfaction;
For my life mortall, Rise from out thy Herse,
And take a life immortall from my Verse.

Delight in Disorder

A sweet disorder in the dresse
Kindles in cloathes a wantonnesse:
A Lawne about the shoulders thrown
Into a fine distraction:
An erring Lace, which here and there
Enthralls the Crimson Stomacher:
A Cuffe neglectfull, and thereby
Ribbands to flow confusedly:
A winning wave (deserving Note)
In the tempestuous petticote:
A carelesse shooe-string, in whose tye
I see a wilde civility:
Doe more bewitch me, then when Art
Is too precise in every part.

To Dean-bourn, a rude River in Devon, by which sometimes he lived

Dean-bourn, farewell; I never look to see
Deane, or thy warty incivility.
Thy rockie bottome, that doth teare thy streams,
And makes them frantick, ev'n to all extreames;
To my content, I never sho'd behold,
Were thy streames silver, or thy rocks all gold.
Rockie thou art; and rockie we discover
Thy men; and rockie are thy wayes all over.
O men, O manners; Now, and ever knowne
To be A Rockie Generation!
A people currish; churlish as the seas;
And rude (almost) as rudest Salvages.
With whom I did, and may re-sojourne when
Rockes turn to Rivers, Rivers turn to Men.

To Julia

How rich and pleasing thou my Julia art
In each thy dainty, and peculiar part!
First, for thy Queen-ship on thy head is set
Of flowers a sweet commingled Coronet:
About thy neck a Carkanet is bound,
Made of the Rubie, Pearle and Diamond:
A golden ring, that shines upon thy thumb:
About thy wrist, the rich Dardanium.
Between thy Breasts (then Doune of Swans more white)
There playes the Saphire with the Chrysolite.
No part besides must of thy selfe be known,
But by the Topaz, Opal, Calcedon.

His Cavalier

Give me that man, that dares bestride
The active Sea-horse, & with pride,
Through that huge field of waters ride:
Who, with his looks too, can appease
The ruffling winds and raging Seas,
In mid'st of all their outrages.
This, this a virtuous man can doe,
Saile against Rocks, and split them too;
I! and a world of Pikes passe through.

To the generous Reader

See, and not see; and if thou chance t'espie
Some Aberrations in my Poetry;
Wink at small faults, the greater, ne'rthelesse
Hide, and with them, their Fathers nakedness.
Let's doe our best, our Watch and Ward to keep:
Homer himself, in a long work, may sleep.

To Criticks

Ile write, because Ile give
You Criticks means to live:
For sho'd I not supply
The Cause, th'effect wo'd die.

To Anthea lying in bed

So looks Anthea, when in bed she lyes,
Orecome, or halfe betray'd by Tiffanies:
Like to a Twi-light, or that simpring Dawn,
That Roses shew, when misted o're with Lawn.
Twilight is yet, till that her Lawnes give way;
Which done, that Dawne, turnes then to perfect day.

To Electra

More white then whitest Lillies far,
Or Snow, or whitest Swans you are:
More white then are the whitest Creames,
Or Moone-light tinselling the streames:
More white then Pearls, or Juno's thigh;
Or Pelops Arme of Yvorie.
True, I confesse; such Whites as these
May me delight, not fully please:
Till, like Ixion's Cloud you be
White, warme, and soft to lye with me.

A Lyrick to Mirth

While the milder Fates consent,
Let's enjoy our merryment:
Drink, and dance, and pipe, and play;
Kisse our Dollies night and day:
Crown'd with clusters of the Vine;
Let us sit, and quaffe our wine.
Call on Bacchus; chaunt his praise;
Shake the Thyrse, and bite the Bayes:
Rouze Anacreon from the dead;
And return him drunk to bed:
Sing o're Horace; for ere long
Death will come and mar the song:
Then shall Wilson and Gotiere
Never sing, or play more here.

An Epitaph upon a sober Matron

With blamelesse carriage, I liv'd here,
To'th' (almost) sev'n and fortieth yeare.
Stout sons I had, and those twice three;
One onely daughter lent to me:
The which was made a happy Bride,
But thrice three Moones before she dy'd.
My modest wedlock, that was known
Contented with the bed of one.

An Epitaph upon a child

Virgins promis'd when I dy'd,
That they wo'd each Primrose-tide,
Duely, Morne and Ev'ning, come,
And with flowers dresse my Tomb.
Having promis'd, pay your debts,
Maids, and here strew Violets.

Upon Scobble. Epig.

Scobble for Whoredome whips his wife; and cryes
He'll slit her nose; But blubb'ring, she replyes,
Good Sir, make no more cuts i'th'outward skin,
One slit's enough to let Adultry in.

Upon Glasco. Epig.

Glasco had none, but now some teeth has got;
Which though they furre, will neither ake, or rot.
Six teeth he has, whereof twice two are known
Made of a Haft, that was a Mutton-bone.
Which not for use, but meerly for the sight,
He weares all day, and drawes those teeth at night.

Single life most secure

Suspicion, Discontent, and Strife,
Come in for Dowrie with a Wife.

On himselfe

I feare no Earthly Powers;
But care for crowns of flowers:
And love to have my Beard
With Wine and Oile besmear'd.
This day Ile drowne all sorrow;
Who knowes to live to morrow?

A Ring presented to Julia

Julia, I bring
To thee this Ring,
Made for thy finger fit;
To shew by this,
That our love is
(Or sho'd be) like to it.

Close though it be,
The joynt is free:
So when Love's yoke is on,
It must not gall,
Or fret at all
With hard oppression.

But it must play
Still either way;
And be, too, such a yoke,
As not too wide,
To over-slide;
Or be so strait to choak.

So we, who beare,
This beame, must reare
Our selves to such a height:
As that the stay
Of either may
Create the burden light.

And as this round
Is no where found
To flaw, or else to sever:
So let our love
As endless prove;
And pure as Gold for ever.

To the Detracter

Where others love, and praise my Verses; still
Thy long-black-Thumb-nail marks 'em out for ill:
A fellon take it, or some Whit-flaw come
For to unslate, or to untile that thumb!
But cry thee Mercy: Exercise thy nailes
To scratch or claw, so that thy tongue not railes:
Some numbers prurient are, and some of these
Are wanton with their itch; scratch, and 'twill please.

Julia's Petticoat

Thy Azure Robe, I did behold,
As ayrie as the leaves of gold;
Which erring here, and wandring there,
Pleas'd with transgression ev'ry where:
Sometimes 'two'd pant, and sigh, and heave,
As if to stir it scarce had leave:
But having got it; thereupon,
'Two'd make a brave expansion.
And pounc't with Stars, it shew'd to me
Like a Celestiall Canopie.
Sometimes 'two'd blaze, and then abate,
Like to a flame growne moderate:
Sometimes away 'two'd wildly fling;
Then to thy thighs so closely cling,
That some conceit did melt me downe,
As Lovers fall into a swoone:
And all confus'd, I there did lie
Drown'd in Delights; but co'd not die.
That Leading Cloud, I follow'd still,
Hoping t'ave seene of it my fill;
But ah! I co'd not: sho'd it move
To Life Eternal, I co'd love.

To Musick

Begin to charme, and as thou stroak'st mine eares
With thy enchantment, melt me into tears.
Then let thy active hand scu'd o're thy Lyre:
And make my spirits frantick with the fire.
That done, sink down into a silv'rie straine;
And make me smooth as Balme, and Oile againe.

Corinna's going a Maying

Get up, get up for shame, the Blooming Morne
    Upon her wings presents the god unshorne.
        See how Aurora throwes her faire
        Fresh-quilted colours through the aire:
        Get up, sweet-Slug-a-bed, and see
        The Dew-bespangling Herbe and Tree.
Each Flower has wept, and bow'd toward the East,
Above an houre since; yet you not drest,
        Nay! not so much as out of bed?
        When all the Birds have Mattens seyd,
        And sung their thankfull Hymnes: 'tis sin,
        Nay, profanation to keep in,
When as a thousand Virgins on this day,
Spring, sooner then the Lark, to fetch in May.

Rise; and put on your Foliage, and be seene
To come forth, like the Spring-time, fresh and greene;
        And sweet as Flora. Take no care
        For Jewels for your Gowne, or Haire:
        Feare not; the leaves will strew
        Gemms in abundance upon you:
Besides, the childhood of the Day has kept,
Against you come, some Orient Pearls unwept:
        Come, and receive them while the light
        Hangs on the Dew-locks of the night:
        And Titan on the Eastern hill
        Retires himself, or else stands still
Till you come forth. Wash, dresse, be briefe in praying:
Few Beads are best, when once we goe a Maying.

Come, my Corinna, come; and comming, marke
How each field turns a street; each street a Parke
        Made green, and trimm'd with trees: see how
        Devotion gives each House a Bough,

Or Branch: Each Porch, each doore, ere this,
    An Arke a Tabernacle is
Made up of white-thorn neatly enterwove;
As if here were those cooler shades of love.
    Can such delights be in the street,
    And open fields, and we not see't?
    Come, we'll abroad; and let's obay
    The Proclamation made for May:
And sin no more, as we have done, by staying;
But my Corinna, come, let's goe a Maying.

There's not a budding Boy, or Girle, this day,
But is got up, and gone to bring in May.
    A deale of Youth, ere this, is come
    Back, and with White-thorn laden home.
    Some have dispatcht their Cakes and Creame,
    Before that we have left to dreame:
And some have wept, and woo'd, and plighted Troth,
And chose their Priest, ere we can cast off sloth:
    Many a green-gown has been given;
    Many a kisse, both odde and even:
    Many a glance too has been sent
    From out the eye, Loves Firmament:
Many a jest told of the Keyes betraying
This night, and Locks pickt, yet w'are not a Maying.

Come, let us goe, while we are in our prime;
And take the harmlesse follie of the time.
    We shall grow old apace, and die
    Before we know our liberty.
    Our life is short; and our dayes run
    As fast away as do's the Sunne:
And as a vapour, or a drop of raine
Once lost, can ne'r be found againe:
    So when or you or I are made
    A fable, song, or fleeting shade;

All love, all liking, all delight
Lies drown'd with us in endlesse night.
Then while time serves, and we are but decaying;
Come, my Corinna, come, let's goe a Maying.

On Julia's breath

Breathe, Julia, breathe, and Ile protest,
   Nay more, Ile deeply sweare,
That all the Spices of the East
   Are circumfused there.

The Lilly in a Christal

You have beheld a smiling Rose
　　　When Virgins hands have drawn
　　　O'r it a Cobweb-Lawne:
And here, you see, this Lilly shows,
　　　Tomb'd in a Christal stone,
More faire in this transparent case,
　　　Then when it grew alone;
　　　And had but single grace.

You see how Creame but naked is;
　　　Nor daunces in the eye
　　　Without a Strawberrie:
Or some fine tincture, like to this,
　　　Which draws the sight thereto,
More by that wantoning with it;
　　　Then when the paler hieu
　　　No mixture did admit.

You see how Amber through the streams
　　　More gently stroaks the sight,
　　　With some conceal'd delight;
Then when he darts his radiant beams
　　　Into the boundlesse aire:
Where either too much light his worth
　　　Doth all at once impaire,
　　　Or set it little forth.

Put Purple Grapes, or Cherries in-
　　　To Glasse, and they will send
　　　More beauty to commend
Them, from that cleane and subtile skin,
　　　Then if they naked stood,
And had no other pride at all,
　　　But their own flesh and blood,
　　　And tinctures naturall.

Thus Lillie, Rose, Grape, Cherry, Creame,
    And Straw-berry do stir
    More love, when they transfer
A weak, a soft, a broken beame;
    Then if they sho'd discover
At full their proper excellence;
    Without some Scean cast over,
    To juggle with the sense.

Thus let this Christal'd Lillie be
    A Rule, how far to teach,
    Your nakednesse must reach:
And that, no further, then we see
    Those glaring colours laid
By Arts wise hand, but to this end
    They sho'd obey a shade;
    Lest they too far extend.

So though y'are white as Swan, or Snow,
    And have the power to move
    A world of men to love:
Yet, when your Lawns & Silks shal flow;
    And that white cloud divide
Into a doubtful Twi-light; then,
    Then will your hidden Pride
    Raise greater fires in men.

To the Virgins, to make much of Time

Gather ye Rose-buds while ye may,
    Old Time is still a flying:
And this same flower that smiles to day,
    To morrow will be dying.

The glorious Lamp of Heaven, the Sun,
    The higher he's a getting;
The sooner will his Race be run,
    An neerer he's to Setting.

That Age is best, which is the first,
    When Youth and Blood are warmer;
But being spent, the worse, and worst
    Times, still succeed the former.

Then be not coy, but use your time;
    And while ye may, goe marry:
For having lost but once your prime,
    You may for ever tarry.

To his Friend, on the untuneable Times

Play I co'd once; but (gentle friend) you see
My Harp hung up, here on the Willow tree.
Sing I co'd once; and bravely too enspire
(With luscious Numbers) my melodious Lyre.
Draw I co'd once (although not stocks or stones,
Amphion-like) men made of flesh and bones,
Whether I wo'd; but (ah!) I know not how,
I feele in me, this transmutation now.
Griefe, (my deare friend) has first my Harp unstrung;
Wither'd my hand, and palsie-struck my tongue.

Upon Julia's breasts

Display thy breasts, my Julia, there let me
Behold that circummortall purity;
Betweene whose glories, there my lips Ile lay,
Ravisht, in that faire *Via Lactea*.

The comming of good luck

So Good-luck came, and on my roofe did light,
Like noyse-lesse Snow; or as the dew of night:
Not all at once, but gently, as the trees
Are, by the Sun-beams, tickel'd by degrees.

The Hock-cart, or Harvest home: To the Right Honourable, Mildmay, Earle of Westmorland

Come Sons of Summer, by whose toile,
We are the Lords of Wine and Oile:
By whose tough labours, and rough hands,
We rip up first, then reap our lands.
Crown'd with the eares of corne, now come,
And, to the Pipe, sing Harvest home.
Come forth, my Lord, and see the Cart
Drest up with all the Country Art.
See, here a Maukin, there a sheet,
As spotlesse pure, as it is sweet:
The Horses, Mares, and frisking Fillies,
(Clad, all, in Linnen, white as Lillies.)
The Harvest Swaines, and Wenches bound
For joy, to see the Hock-cart crown'd.
About the Cart, heare, how the Rout
Of Rurall Younglings raise the shout;
Pressing before, some coming after,
Those with a shout, and these with laughter.
Some blesse the Cart; some kisse the sheaves;
Some prank them up with Oaken leaves:
Some crosse the Fill-horse; some with great
Devotion, stroak the home-borne wheat:
While other Rusticks, lesse attent
To Prayers, then to Merryment,
Run after with their breeches rent.
Well, on, brave boyes, to your Lords Hearth,
Glitt'ring with fire; where, for your mirth,
Ye shall see first the large and cheefe
Foundation of your Feast, Fat Beefe:
With Upper Stories, Mutton, Veale
And Bacon, (which makes full the meale)
With sev'rall dishes standing by,

As here a Custard, there a Pie,
And here all tempting Frumentie.
And for to make the merry cheere,
If smirking Wine be wanting here,
There's that, which drowns all care, stout Beere:
Which freely drink to your Lords health,
Then to the Plough, (the Common-wealth)
Next to your Flailes, your Fanes, your Fatts;
Then to the Maids with Wheaten Hats:
To the rough Sickle, and crookt Sythe,
Drink frollick boyes, till all be blythe.
Feed, and grow fat; and as ye eat,
Be mindfull, that the lab'ring Neat
(As you) may have their fill of meat.
And know, besides, ye must revoke
The patient Oxe unto the Yoke,
And all goe back unto the Plough
And Harrow, (though they'r hang'd up now.)
And, you must know, your Lords word's true,
Feed him ye must, whose food fils you.
And that this pleasure is like raine,
Not sent ye for to drowne your paine,
But for to make it spring againe.

To Meddowes

Ye have been fresh and green,
　　Ye have been fill'd with flowers:
And ye the Walks have been
　　Where Maids have spent their houres.

You have beheld, how they
　　With Wicker Arks did come
To kisse, and beare away
　　The richer Couslips home.

Y'ave heard them sweetly sing,
　　And seen them in a Round:
Each Virgin, like a Spring,
　　With Hony-succles crown'd.

But now, we see, none here,
　　Whose silv'rie feet did tread,
And with dishevell'd Haire,
　　Adorn'd this smoother Mead.

Like Unthrifts, having spent,
　　Your stock, and needy grown,
Y'are left here to lament
　　Your poore estates, alone.

To his Household gods

Rise, Household-gods, and let us goe;
But whither, I my selfe not know.
First, let us dwell on rudest seas;
Next, with severest Salvages;
Last, let us make our best abode,
Where humane foot, as yet, ne'r trod:
Search worlds of Ice; and rather there
Dwell, then in lothed Devonshire.

To the Nightingale, and Robin-Red-brest

When I departed am, ring thou my knell,
Thou pittifull, and pretty Philomel:
And when I'm laid out for a Corse; then be
Thou Sexton (Red-brest) for to cover me.

The silken Snake

For sport my Julia threw a Lace
Of silke and silver at my face:
Watchet the silke was; and did make
A shew, as if't'ad been a snake:
The suddenness did me affright;
But though it scar'd, it did not bite.

To all young men that love

I could wish you all, who love,
That ye could your thoughts remove
From your Mistresses, and be,
Wisely wanton (like to me.)
I could wish you dispossest
Of that Fiend that marres your rest;
And with Tapers comes to fright
Your weake senses in the night.
I co'd wish, ye all, who frie
Cold as Ice, or coole as I.

No fault in women

No fault in women to refuse
The offer, which they most wo'd chuse.
No fault in women, to confesse
How tedious they are in their dresse.
No fault in women, to lay on
The tincture of Vermillion:
And there to give the cheek a die
Of white, where nature doth deny.
No fault in women, to make show
Of largeness, when th'are nothing so:
(When true it is, the out-side swels
With inward Buckram, little else.)
No fault in women, though they be
But seldome from suspition free:
No fault in womankind, at all,
If they but slip, and never fall.

Upon Shark. Epig.

Shark, when he goes to any publick feast,
Eates to ones thinking, of all there, the least.
What saves the master of the House thereby?
When if the servants search, they may descry
In his wide Codpeece, (dinner being done)
Two Napkins cram'd up, and a silver Spoone.

Bashfulnesse

Of all our parts, the eyes expresse
The sweetest kind of bashfulnesse.

Upon Prudence Baldwin her sicknesse

Prue, my dearest Maid, is sick,
Almost to be Lunatick:
Æsculapius! come and bring
Means for her recovering;
And a gallant Cock shall be
Offer'd up by Her, to Thee.

To Daffadills

Faire Daffadills, we weep to see
    You haste away so soone:
As yet the early-rising Sun
    Has not attain'd his Noone.
            Stay, stay,
        Untill the hasting day
                Has run
        But to the Even-song;
And, having pray'd together, we
        Will goe with you along.

We have short time to stay, as you,
    We have as short a Spring;
As quick a growth to meet Decay,
    As you, or any thing.
            We die,
        As your hours doe, and drie
                Away,
        Like to the Summers raine;
Or as the pearles of Mornings dew
        Ne'r to be found againe.

The Bracelet to Julia

Why I tye about thy wrist,
Julia, this my silken twist;
For what other reason is't,
But to shew thee how in part,
Thou my pretty Captive art?
But thy Bondslave is my heart:
'Tis but silke that bindeth thee,
Knap the thread, and thou art free:
But 'tis otherwise with me;
I am bound, and fast bound so,
That from thee I cannot go;
If I co'd, I wo'd not so.

The departure of the good Dæmon

What can I do in Poetry,
Now the good Spirit's gone from me?
Why nothing now, but lonely sit,
And over-read what I have writ.

The power in the people

Let Kings Command, and doe the best they may,
The saucie Subjects still will beare the sway.

On Julia's Picture

How am I ravisht! When I do but see,
The Painters art in thy Sciography?
If so, how much more shall I dote thereon,
When once he gives it incarnation?

Her Bed

See'st thou that Cloud as silver cleare,
Plump, soft, & swelling every where?
Tis *Julia's* Bed, and she sleeps there.

Her Legs

Fain would I kiss my Julia's dainty Leg,
Which is as white and hair-less as an egge.

Upon Judith. Epig.

Judith has cast her old-skin, and got new;
And walks fresh varnisht to the publick view.
Foule Judith was; and foule she will be known,
For all this fair Transfiguration.

To the most fair and lovely Mistris, Anne Soame, now Lady Abdie

So smell those odours that do rise
From out the wealthy spiceries:
So smels the flowre of blooming Clove;
Or Roses smother'd in the stove:
So smells the Aire of spiced wine;
Or Essences of Jessimine:
So smells the Breath about the hives,
When well the work of hony thrives;
And all the busie Factours come
Laden with wax and hony home:
So smell those neat and woven Bowers,
All over-archt with Oringe flowers,
And Almond blossoms, that do mix
To make rich these Aromatikes:
So smell those bracelets, and those bands
Of Amber chaf't between the hands,
When thus enkindled they transpire
A noble perfume from the fire.
The wine of cherries, and to these,
The cooling breath of Respasses;
The smell of mornings milk, and cream;
Butter of Cowslips mixt with them;
Of rosted warden, or bak'd peare,
These are not to be reckon'd here;
When as the meanest part of her,
Smells like the maiden-Pomander.
Thus sweet she smells, or what can be
More lik'd by her, or lov'd by mee.

Upon M. Ben. Johnson. Epig.

After the rare Arch-Poet JOHNSON dy'd,
The Sock grew loathsome, and the Buskins pride,
Together with the Stages glory stood
Each like a poore and pitied widowhood.
The Cirque prophan'd was; and all postures rackt:
For men did strut, and stride, and stare, not act.
Then temper flew from words; and men did squeake,
Looke red, and blow, and bluster, but not speake:
No Holy-Rage, or frantick-fires did stirre,
Or flash about the spacious Theater.
No clap of hands, or shout, or praises-proofe
Did crack the Play-house sides, or cleave her roofe.
Artlesse the Sceane was; and that monstrous sin
Of deep and arrant ignorance came in;
Such ignorance as theirs was, who once hist
At thy unequal'd Play, the Alchymist:
Oh fie upon 'em! Lastly too, all witt
In utter darkenes did, and still will sit
Sleeping the lucklesse Age out, till that she
Her Resurrection ha's again with Thee.

To his Nephew, to be prosperous in his art of Painting

On, as thou hast begunne, brave youth, and get
The Palme from Urbin, Titian, Tintarret,
Brugel and Coxie, and the workes out-doe,
Of Holben, and That mighty Ruben too.
So draw, and paint, as none may do the like,
No, not the glory of the World, Vandike.

To his maid Prew

These Summer-Birds did with thy Master stay
The times of warmth; but then they flew away;
Leaving their Poet (being now grown old)
Expos'd to all the comming Winters cold.
But thou kind Prew did'st with my Fates abide,
As well the Winters, as the Summers Tide:
For which thy Love, live with thy Master here,
Not two, but all the seasons of the yeare.

Clothes do but cheat and cousen us

Away with silks, away with Lawn,
Ile have no Sceans, or Curtains drawn:
Give me my Mistresse, as she is,
Drest in her nak't simplicities:
For as my Heart, ene so mine Eye
Is wone with flesh, not *Drapery*.

To Dianeme

Shew me thy feet; shew me thy legs, thy thighes;
Shew me Those Fleshie Principalities;
Shew me that Hill (where smiling Love doth sit)
Having a living Fountain under it.
Shew me thy waste; Then let me there withall,
By the Assention of thy Lawn, see All.

Upon Julia's unlacing her self

Tell, if thou canst, (and truly) whence doth come
This Camphire, Storax, Spiknard, Galbanum:
These Musks, these Ambers, and those other smells
(Sweet as the Vestrie of the Oracles.)
Ile tell thee; while my Julia did unlace
Her silken bodies, but a breathing space:
The passive Aire such odour then assum'd,
As when to Jove Great Juno goes perfum'd.
Whose pure-Immortall body doth transmit
A scent, that fills both Heaven and Earth with it.

To Sycamores

I'm sick of Love; O let me lie
Under your shades, to sleep or die!
Either is welcome; so I have
Or here my Bed, or here my Grave.
Why do you sigh, and sob, and keep
Time with the tears, that I do weep?
Say, have ye sence, or do you prove
What Crucifixions are in Love?
I know ye do; and that's the why,
You sigh for Love, as well as I.

To Daisies, not to shut so soone

Shut not so soon; the dull-ey'd night
   Ha's not as yet begunne
To make a seisure on the light,
   Or to seale up the Sun.

No Marigolds yet closed are;
   No shadowes great appeare;
Nor doth the early Shepheards Starre
   Shine like a spangle here.

Stay but till my Julia close
   Her life-begetting eye;
And let the whole world then dispose
   It selfe to live or dye.

To Julia in the Temple

Besides us two, i'th'Temple here's not one
To make up now a Congregation.
Let's to the Altar of perfumes then go,
And say short Prayers; and when we have done so,
Then we shall see, how in a little space,
Saints will come in to fill each Pew and Place.

Upon himself

Come, leave this loathed Country-life, and then
Grow up to be a Roman Citizen.
Those mites of Time, which yet remain unspent,
Waste thou in that most Civill Government.
Get their comportment, and the gliding tongue
Of those mild Men, thou art to live among:
Then being seated in that smoother Sphere,
Decree thy everlasting Topick there.
And to the Farm-house nere return at all;
Though Granges do not love thee, Cities shall.

To the right Honourable Mildmay, Earle of Westmorland

You are a Lord, an Earle, nay more, a Man,
Who writes sweet Numbers well as any can:
If so, why then are not These Verses hurld,
Like Sybels Leaves, throughout the ample world?
What is a Jewell if it be not set
Forth by a Ring, or some rich Carkanet?
But being so; then the beholders cry,
See, see a Jemme (as rare as Bælus eye.)
Then publick praise do's runne upon the Stone,
For a most rich, a rare, a precious One.
Expose your jewels then unto the view,
That we may praise Them, or themselves prize You.
Vertue conceal'd (with Horace you'l confesse)
Differs not much from drowzie slothfullnesse.

Upon Julia's haire fill'd with Dew

Dew sate on Julia's haire,
    And spangled too,
Like Leaves that laden are
    With trembling Dew:
Or glitter'd to my sight,
    As when the Beames
Have their reflected light,
    Daunc't by the Streames.

Another on her

How can I choose but love, and follow her,
Whose shadow smels like milder Pomander!
How can I chuse but kisse her, whence do's come
The *Storax*, *Spiknard*, *Myrrhe*, and *Ladanum*.

Fresh Cheese and Cream

Wo'd yee have fresh Cheese and Cream?
Julia's Breast can give you them:
And if more; Each Nipple cries,
To your Cream, here's Strawberries.

To a Bed of Tulips

Bright Tulips, we do know,
You had your comming hither;
And Fading-time do's show,
That Ye must quickly wither.

Your Sister-hoods may stay,
And smile here for your houre;
But dye ye must away:
Even as the meanest Flower.

Come Virgins then, and see
Your frailties; and bemone ye;
For lost like these, 'twill be,
As Time had never known ye.

Upon Jack and Jill. Epig.

When Jill complaines to Jack for want of meate;
Jack kisses Jill, and bids her freely eate:
Jill sayes, of what? sayes Jack, on that sweet kisse,
Which full of Nectar and Ambrosia is,
The food of Poets; so I thought sayes Jill,
That makes them looke so lanke, so Ghost-like still.
Let Poets feed on aire, or what they will;
Let me feed full, till that I fart, sayes Jill.

To Julia

Julia, when thy Herrick dies,
Close thou up thy Poets eyes:
And his last breath, let it be
Taken in by none but Thee.

To his Kinswoman, Mistresse Susanna Herrick

When I consider (Dearest) thou dost stay
But here awhile, to languish and decay;
Like to these Garden-glories, which here be
The Flowrie-sweet resemblances of Thee:
With griefe of heart, methinks, I thus doe cry,
Wo'd thou hast ne'r been born, or might'st not die.

Upon her feet

Her pretty feet
Like snailes did creep
A little out, and then,
As if they started at Bo-peep,
Did soon draw in agen.

Upon his gray haires

Fly me not, though I be gray,
Lady, this I know you'l say;
Better look the Roses red,
When with white commingled.
Black your haires are; mine are white;
This begets the more delight,
When things meet most opposite:
As in Pictures we descry,
Venus standing Vulcan by.

Anacreontike

Born I was to be old,
   And for to die here:
After that, in the mould
   Long for to lye here.
But before that day comes,
   Still I be Bousing;
For I know, in the Tombs
   There's no Carousing.

Meat without mirth

Eaten I have; and though I had good cheere,
I did not sup, because no friends were there.
Where Mirth and Friends are absent when we Dine
Or Sup, there wants the Incense and the Wine.

An Ode to Sir Clipsebie Crew

Here we securely live, and eate
    The Creame of meat;
  And keep eternal fires,
By which we sit, and doe Divine
      As Wine
    And Rage inspires.

If full we charme; then call upon
    Anacreon
  To grace the frantick Thyrse:
And having drunk, we raise a shout
      Throughout
    To praise his Verse.

Then cause we Horace to be read,
    Which sung, or seyd,
  A Goblet, to the brim,
Of Lyrick Wine, both swell'd and crown'd,
      A Round
    We quaffe to him.

Thus, thus, we live, and spend the houres
    In Wine and Flowers:
  And make the frollick yeere,
The Month, the Week, the instant Day
      To stay
    The longer here.

Come then, brave Knight, and see the Cell
    Wherein I dwell;
  And my Enchantments too;
Which Love and noble freedome is;
      And this
    Shall fetter you.

Take Horse, and come; or be so kind,
        To send your mind
    (Though but in Numbers few)
And I shall think I have the heart,
        Or part
    Of Clipseby Crew.

To his Tomb-maker

Go I must; when I am gone,
Write but this upon my Stone;
Chaste I liv'd, without a wife,
That's the Story of my life.
Strewings need none, every flower
Is in this word, Batchelour.

Pitie to the prostrate

Tis worse then barbarous cruelty to show
No part of pitie on a conquer'd foe.

His content in the Country

Here, here I live with what my Board,
Can with the smallest cost afford.
Though ne'r so mean the Viands be,
They well content my Prew and me.
Or Pea, or Bean, or Wort, or Beet,
What ever comes, content makes sweet:
Here we rejoyce, because no Rent
We pay for our poore Tenement:
Wherein we rest, and never feare
The Landlord, or the Usurer.
The Quarter-day do's ne'r affright
Our Peacefull slumbers in the night.
We eate our own, and batten more,
Because we feed on no mans score:
But pitie those, whose flanks grow great,
Swel'd with the Lard of others meat.
We blesse our Fortunes, when we see
Our own beloved privacie:
And like our living, where w'are known
To very few, or else to none.

The credit of the Conquerer

He who commends the vanquisht, speaks the Power,
And glorifies the worthy Conquerer.

Art above Nature, to Julia

When I behold a Forrest spread
With silken trees upon thy head;
And when I see that other Dresse
Of flowers set in comlinesse:
When I behold another grace
In the ascent of curious Lace,
Which like a Pinacle doth shew
The top, and the top-gallant too.
Then, when I see thy Tresses bound
Into an Ovall, square, or round;
And knit in knots far more then I
Can tell by tongue; or true-love tie:
Next, when those Lawnie Filmes I see
Play with a wild civility:
And all those airie silks to flow,
Alluring me, and tempting so:
I must confesse, mine eye and heart
Dotes less on Nature, then on Art.

Upon Urles. Epig.

Urles had the Gout so, that he co'd not stand;
Then from his Feet, it shifted to his Hand:
When 'twas in's Feet, his Charity was small;
Now tis in's Hand, he gives no Almes at all.

Upon a free Maid, with a foule breath

You say you'l kiss me, and I thanke you for it:
But stinking breath, I do as hell abhorre it.

Upon the troublesome times

O! times most bad,
Without the scope
   Of hope
Of better to be had!

Where shall I goe,
Or whither run
   To shun
This publique overthrow?

No places are
(This I am sure)
   Secure
In this our wasting Warre.

Some storms w'ave past;
Yet we must all
   Down fall,
And perish at the last.

His Prayer to Ben. Johnson

When I a Verse shall make,
Know I have praid thee,
For old Religions sake,
Saint Ben to aide me.

Make the way smooth for me,
When I, thy Herrick,
Honouring thee, on my knee
Offer my Lyrick.

Candles Ile give to thee,
And a new Altar;
And thou Saint Ben, shalt be
Writ in my Psalter.

The Night-piece, to Julia

Her Eyes the Glow-worme lend thee,
The Shooting Starres attend thee;
   And the Elves also,
   Whose little eyes glow,
Like the sparks of fire, befriend thee.

No Will-o'th'-Wispe mis-light thee;
Nor Snake, or Slow-worme bite thee:
   But on, on thy way
   Not making a stay,
Since Ghost ther's none to affright thee.

Let not the darke thee cumber;
What though the Moon do's slumber?
   The Starres of the night
   Will lend thee their light,
Like Tapers cleare without number.

Then Julia let me wooe thee,
Thus, thus to come unto me:
   And when I shall meet
   Thy silv'ry feet,
My soule Ile poure into thee.

The Country life, to the honoured M. End. Porter, Groome of the Bed-Chamber to His Maj.

Sweet Country life, to such unknown,
Whose lives are others, not their own!
But serving Courts, and Cities, be
Less happy, less enjoying thee.
Thou never Plow'st the Oceans foame
To seek, and bring rough Pepper home:
Nor to the Eastern Ind dost rove
To bring from thence the scorched Clove.
Nor, with the losse of thy lov'd rest,
Bring'st home the Ingot from the West.
No, thy Ambition's Master-piece
Flies no thought higher then a fleece:
Or how to pay thy Hinds, and cleere
All scores; and so to end the yeere:
But walk'st about thine own dear bounds,
Not envying others larger grounds:
For well thou know'st, 'tis not th'extent
Of Land makes life, but sweet content.
When now the Cock (the Plow-mans Horne)
Calls forth the lilly-wristed Morne;
Then to thy corn-fields thou dost goe,
Which though well soyl'd, yet thou dost know,
That the best compost for the Lands
Is the wise Masters Feet, and Hands.
There at the Plough thou find'st thy Teame,
With a Hind whistling there to them:
And cheer'st them up, by singing how
The Kingdoms portion is the Plow.
This done, then to th'enameld Meads
Thou go'st; and as thy foot there treads,
Thou seest a present God-like Power
Imprinted in each Herbe and Flower:

And smell'st the breath of great-ey'd Kine,
Sweet as the blossomes of the Vine.
Here thou behold'st thy large sleek Neat
Unto the Dew-laps up in meat:
And, as thou look'st, the wanton Steere,
The Heifer, Cow, and Oxe draw neere
To make a pleasing pastime there.
These seen, thou go'st to view thy flocks
Of sheep, (safe from the Wolfe and Fox)
And find'st their bellies there as full
Of short sweet grasse, as backs with wool.
And leav'st them (as they feed and fill)
A Shepherd piping on a hill.
For Sports, for Pagentrie, and Playes,
Thou hast thy Eves, and Holydayes:
On which the young men and maids meet,
To exercise their dancing feet:
Tripping the comely country round,
With Daffadils and Daisies crown'd.
Thy Wakes, thy Quintels, here thou hast,
Thy May-poles too with Garlands grac't:
Thy Morris-dance; thy Whitsun-ale;
Thy Sheering-feast, which never faile.
Thy Harvest home; thy Wassaile bowle,
That's tost up after Fox i'th'Hole.
Thy Mummeries; thy Twelfe-tide Kings
And Queenes; thy Christmas revellings:
Thy Nut-browne mirth; thy Russet wit;
And no man payes too deare for it.
To these, thou hast thy times to goe
And trace the Hare i'th'trecherous Snow:
Thy witty wiles to draw, and get
The Larke into the Trammell net:
Thou hast thy Cockrood, and thy Glade
To take the precious Phesant made:
Thy Lime-twigs, Snares, and Pit-falls then

To catch the pilfring Birds, not Men.
O happy life! if that their good
The Husbandmen but understood!
Who all the day themselves doe please,
And Younglings, with such sports as these.
And, lying down, have nought t'affright
Sweet sleep, that makes more short the night.
                    Cætera desunt——

What kind of Mistresse he would have

Be the Mistresse of my choice,
Cleane in manners, cleere in voice:
Be she witty, more then wise;
Pure enough, though not Precise:
Be she shewing in her dresse,
Like a civill Wilderness;
That the curious may detect
Order in a sweet neglect:
Be she rowling in her eye,
Tempting all the passers by:
And each Ringlet of her haire,
An Enchantment, or a Snare,
For to catch the Lookers on;
But her self held fast by none.
Let her Lucrece all day be,
Thais in the night, to me.
Be she such, as neither will
Famish me, nor over-fill.

The Rainbow: or curious Covenant

Mine eyes, like clouds, were drizling raine,
And as they thus did entertaine
The gentle Beams from Julia's sight
To mine eyes level'd opposite:
O Thing admir'd! there did appeare
A curious Rainbow smiling there;
Which was the Covenant, that she
No more wo'd drown mine eyes, or me.

His returne to London

From the dull confines of the drooping West,
To see the day spring from the pregnant East,
Ravisht in spirit, I come, nay more, I flie
To thee, blest place of my Nativitie!
Thus, thus with hallowed foot I touch the ground,
With thousand blessings by the Fortune crown'd.
O fruitfull Genius! that bestowest here
An everlasting plenty, yeere by yeere.
O Place! O People! Manners! fram'd to please
All Nations, Customes, Kindreds, Languages!
I am a free-born Roman; suffer then,
That I amongst you live a Citizen.
London my home is: though by hard fate sent
Into a long and irksome banishment;
Yet since cal'd back; henceforward let me be,
O native countrey, repossest by thee!
For, rather then I'le to the West return,
I'le beg of thee first here to have mine Urn.
Weak I am grown, and must in short time fall;
Give thou my sacred Reliques Buriall.

Not every day fit for Verse

'Tis not ev'ry day, that I
Fitted am to prophesie:
No, but when the Spirit fils
The fantastick Pannicles:
Full of fier; then I write
As the Godhead doth indite.
Thus inrag'd, my lines are hurl'd,
Like the Sybells, through the world.
Look how next the holy fier
Either slakes, or doth retire;
So the Fancie cooles, till when
That brave Spirit comes agen.

His Grange, or private wealth

Though Clock,
To tell how night drawes hence, I've none,
A Cock,
I have, to sing how day drawes on.
I have
A maid (my Prew) by good luck sent,
To save
That little, Fates me gave or lent.
A Hen
I keep, which creeking day by day,
Tells when
She goes her long white egg to lay.
A goose
I have, which, with a jealous eare,
Lets loose
Her tongue, to tell what danger's neare.
A Lamb
I keep (tame) with my morsells fed,
Whose Dam
An Orphan left him (lately dead.)
A Cat
I keep, that playes about my House,
Grown fat,
With eating many a miching Mouse.
To these
A Trasy I do keep, whereby
I please
The more my rurall privacie:
Which are
But toyes, to give my heart some ease:
Where care
None is, slight things do lightly please.

Up tailes all

        Begin with a kisse,
        Go on too with this:
And thus, thus, thus let us smother
        Our lips for a while,
        But let's not beguile
Our hope of one for the other.

        This play, be assur'd,
        Long enough has endur'd,
Since more and more is exacted;
        For love he doth call
        For his Uptailes all;
And that's the part to be acted.

The Wake

Come Anthea let us two
Go to Feast, as others do.
Tarts and Custards, Creams and Cakes,
Are the Junketts still at Wakes:
Unto which the Tribes resort,
Where the businesse is the sport:
Morris-dancers thou shalt see,
Marian too in Pagentrie:
And a Mimick to devise
Many grinning properties.
Players there will be, and those
Base in action as in clothes:
Yet with strutting they will please
The incurious Villages.
Neer the dying of the day,
There will be a Cudgell-Play,
Where a Coxcomb will be broke,
Ere a good word can be spoke:
But the anger ends all here,
Drencht in Ale, or drown'd in Beere.
Happy Rusticks, best content
With the cheapest Merriment:
And possesse no other feare,
Then to want the Wake next Yeare.
By silent Nights, and the
Three Formes of Heccate:
By all Aspects that blesse
The sober Sorceresse,
While juice she straines, and pith
To make her Philters with:
By Time, that hastens on
Things to perfection:
And by your self, the best

Conjurement of the rest:
O my Electra! be
In love with none, but me.

Upon Julia's Clothes

When as in silks my Julia goes,
Then, then (me thinks) how sweetly flowes
That liquefaction of her clothes.

Next, when I cast mine eyes and see
That brave Vibration each way free;
O how that glittering taketh me!

Upon Prew his Maid

In this little Urne is laid
Prewdence Baldwin (once my maid)
From whose happy spark here let
Spring the purple Violet.

To M. Henry Lawes, the excellent
Composer of his Lyricks

Touch but thy Lire (my Harrie) and I heare
From thee some raptures of the rare Gotire.
Then if thy voice commingle with the String
I heare in thee rare Laniere to sing;
Or curious Wilson: Tell me, canst thou be
Less then Apollo, that usurp'st such Three?
Three, unto whom the whole world give applause;
Yet their Three praises, praise but One; that's Lawes.

Kings and Tyrants

'Twixt Kings & Tyrants there's this difference known;
Kings seek their Subjects good: Tyrants their owne.

Kisses Loathsome

I abhor the slimie kisse,
(Which to me most loathsome is.)
Those lips please me which are plac't
Close, but not too strictly lac't:
Yeilding I wo'd have them; yet
Not a wimbling Tongue admit:
What sho'd poking-sticks make there,
When the ruffe is set elsewhere?

Upon Julia's haire, bundled up in a golden net

Tell me, what needs those rich deceits,
These golden Toyles, and Trammel-nets,
To take thine haires when they are knowne
Already tame, and all thine owne?
'Tis I am wild, and more then haires
Deserve these Mashes and those snares.
Set free thy Tresses, let them flow
As aires doe breathe, or winds doe blow:
And let such curious Net-works be
Lesse set for them, then spred for me.

Julia's Churching, or Purification

Put on thy Holy Fillitings, and so
To th'Temple with the sober Midwife go.
Attended thus (in a most solemn wise)
By those who serve the Child-bed misteries.
Burn first thine incense; next, when as thou see'st
The candid Stole thrown ore the Pious Priest;
With reverend Curtsies come, and to him bring
Thy free (and not decurted) offering.
All Rites well ended, with faire Auspice come
(As to the breaking of a Bride-Cake) home:
Where ceremonious Hymen shall for thee
Provide a second Epithalamie.
She who keeps chastly to her husbands side
Is not for one, but every night his Bride:
And stealing still with love, and feare to Bed,
Brings him not one, but many a Maiden-head.

The Hony-combe

If thou hast found an honie-combe,
Eate thou not all, but taste on some:
For if thou eat'st it to excess;
That sweetness turnes to Loathsomness.
Taste it to Temper; then 'twill be
Marrow, and Manna unto thee.

Upon Julia's washing her self in the river

How fierce was I, when I did see
My Julia wash her self in thee!
So Lillies thorough Christall look:
So purest pebbles in the brook:
As in the River Julia did,
Halfe with a Lawne of water hid,
Into they streames my self I threw,
And strugling there, I kist thee too;
And more had done (it is confest)
Had not thy waves forbad the rest.

Upon his Spaniell Tracie

Now thou art dead, no eye shall ever see,
For shape and service, Spaniell like to thee.
This shall my love doe, give thy sad death one
Teare, that deserves of me a million.

His tears to Thamasis

I send, I send here my supremest kiss
To thee my silver-footed Thamasis.
No more shall I reiterate thy Strand,
Whereon so many Stately Structures stand:
Nor in the summers sweeter evenings go,
To bath in thee (as thousand others doe.)
No more shall I a long thy christall glide,
In Barge (with boughes and rushes beautifi'd)
With soft-smooth Virgins (for our chast disport)
To Richmond, Kingstone, and to Hampton-Court:
Never againe shall I with Finnie-Ore
Put from, or draw unto the faithfull shore:
And Landing here, or safely Landing there,
Make way to my Beloved Westminster:
Or to the Golden-cheap-side, where the earth
Of Julia Herrick gave to me my Birth.
May all clean Nimphs and curious water Dames,
With Swan-like-state, flote up & down thy streams:
No drought upon thy wanton waters fall
To make them Leane, and languishing at all.
No ruffling winds come hither to discease
Thy pure, and Silver-wristed Naides.
Keep up your state ye streams; and as ye spring,
Never make sick your Banks by surfeiting.
Grow young with Tydes, and though I see ye never,
Receive this vow, so fare-ye-well for ever.

His last request to Julia

I have been wanton, and too bold I feare,
To chafe o're much the Virgins cheek or eare:
Beg for my Pardon Julia; He doth winne
Grace with the Gods, who's sorry for his sinne.
That done, my Julia, dearest Julia, come,
And go with me to chuse my Buriall roome:
My Fates are ended; when thy Herrick dyes,
Claspe thou his Book, then close thou up his Eyes.

The end of his worke

Part of the worke remaines; one part is past:
And here my ship rides having Anchor cast.

To Crowne it

My wearied Barke, O Let it now be Crown'd!
The Haven reacht to which I first was bound.

On Himselfe

The worke is done: young men, and maidens set
Upon my curles the Mirtle Coronet,
Washt with sweet ointments; Thus at last I come
To suffer in the Muses Martyrdome:
But with this comfort, if my blood be shed,
The Muses will weare blackes, when I am dead.

The pillar of Fame

Fames pillar here, at last, we set,
Out-during Marble, Brasse, or Jet,
    Charm'd and enchanted so,
    As to withstand the blow
        Of   overthrow:
        Nor shall the seas,
        Or   OUTRAGES
        Of storms orebear
        What we up-rear,
        Tho Kingdoms fal,
    This   pillar   never   shall
    Decline   or   waste   at   all;
But stand for ever by his owne
Firme and well fixt foundation.

To his Book's end this last line he'd have plac't,
Jocond his Muse was; but his Life was chast.

Gods Anger without Affection

God when He's angry here with any one,
His wrath is free from perturbation;
And when we think His looks are sowre and grim,
The alteration is in us, not Him.

Affliction

God n'ere afflicts us more then our desert,
Though He may seem to over-act His part:
Somtimes He strikes us more then flesh can beare;
But yet still lesse then Grace can suffer here.

The Heart

In Prayer the Lips ne're act the winning part,
Without the sweet concurrence of the Heart.

To his sweet Saviour

Night hath no wings, to him that cannot sleep;
And Time seems then, not for to flie, but creep;
Slowly her chariot drives, as if that she
Had broke her wheele, or crackt her axeltree.
Just so it is with me, who list'ning, pray
The winds, to blow the tedious night away;
That I might see the cheerful peeping day.
Sick is my heart; O Saviour! do Thou please
To make my bed soft in my sicknesses:
Lighten my candle, so that I beneath
Sleep not for ever in the vaults of death:
Let me Thy voice betimes i'th morning heare;
Call, and I'le come; say Thou, the when, and where:
Draw me, but first, and after Thee I'le run,
And make no one stop, till my race be done.

To God, on his sicknesse

What though my Harp, and Violl be
Both hung upon the Willow-tree?
What though my bed be now my grave,
And for my house I darknesse have?
What though my healthfull dayes are fled,
And I lie numbred with the dead?
Yet I have hope, by Thy great power,
To spring; though now a wither'd flower.

Tapers

Those Tapers, which we set upon the grave,
In fun'rall pomp, but this importance have;
That soules departed are not put out quite;
But, as they walk't here in their vestures white,
So live in Heaven, in everlasting light.

Advice to a Maid

Loue in thy youth fayre Mayde bee wise
    Ould time will make thee colder
and thoughe each Morneinge newe arise
    yett wee each daye growe oulder,

Thou as heauen art faire, and younge,
    thine Eyes like twynn Starrs shineinge,
but ere an other daye bee sprunge
    all theise will bee declineinge.

Then winter comes with all his feares,
    and all thy sweetes shall borrowe,
too Late then wilt thou showre thy teares,
    and I too Late shall sorrowe.

Epitaph on the Tomb of Sir Edward Giles and his wife in the South Aisle of Dean Prior Church

No trust to Metals nor to Marbles, when
These have their Fate, and wear away as Men;
Times, Titles, Trophies, may be lost and Spent;
But Vertue Rears the eternal Monument.
What more than these can Tombs or Tomb-stones Say
But here's the Sun-set of a Tedious day:
These Two asleep are: I'll but be Vndrest
And so to Bed: Pray wish us all Good Rest.